RISING ABOVE ALL ODDS

THE MEMOIR OF AN IMMIGRANT

IN NEW YORK CITY

SHARON D. CHARLES

RISING ABOVE ALL ODDS

THE MEMOIR OF AN IMMIGRANT

IN NEW YORK CITY

Sharon D. Charles

Dedication

In loving memory of my mom

Mrs. Mavis Frederick nee Charles

I want to thank the following wonderful people I have met throughout my life in this country, USA, which I call home: Tamar Bryk, Hillel Bryk, Michael Samuel, Dr. Nancy Lester, Dr. George Irish, Marlene Ledford, Eunice Rodrick, James Johnson Marjorie Chase and Alvin Knight

Published by **Caribbean Diaspora Press Inc**
718-617-3744   irishjag519@gmail.com

ISBN   978-0-692-89102-5

Printed in USA

Contact:
Sharon D. Charles (A proud Medgar Evers College Graduate)
Email: guava42@aol.com

PROLOGUE

As a college student and employee, I live a very busy life. I find myself studying hard and completing all assignments on time. When I am not working or attending classes, I use my pastime reading, cooking, and going to the movies. I enjoy long walks in the park and crocheting. I also enjoy watching basketball games on Television. The New York Knicks is my favorite team. Although, they give me heart burn when they are knocked out of the playoffs, I love them dearly. I enjoy reading novels especially mysteries and love stories. I also love reading about world news and politics. I find it is fascinating and interesting to know what is happening in other countries around the world. I try my best to keep up to date with the local news and politics. I believe it is essential to understand what is going on around you because with that knowledge, you will be prepared to handle any situation that comes your way.

Bachelor's Graduation 2014

CONTENTS

August 1982

Bridgetown Barbados

arles winning at C A C games

Winning the CAC Games

Sharon D. Charles 302

Chapter One

Hometown Days

I was born on the beautiful Caribbean island of Grenada, also known as the Island of Spice due to its production of the spices nutmeg and mace. It is one of the most beautiful small islands in the region. The Grenadian people are caring, friendly and generous. I grew up in a small town in the parish of St. John's, which is best known for it large fishing industry and night life. The town of "Gouyave," derived from the word guava, is one of the most exciting places in the country. Its often being referred to as the town that never sleeps. With clear blue sea water along its beaches, fresh fish, loving people, and profuse sunshine, there is an endless set of activities for everyone.

I came from a poor family but was determined to make my mother proud. My family structure was very supportive; although my parents were not rich, they made love the central focus of my upbringing, which I think is largely responsible for the person I am today. Honesty was also an important value which my family treasured. Consequently, we placed high value on trusted relationships among family and friends.

Throughout my high school career, I was an active sports figure, playing netball, running track and marathons. I was excellent in track and actually gained the respect from the community where I grew up, because I represented Grenada during competition against other Caribbean Islands. One of my memorable games was the Central American & Caribbean Games in Cuba in 1982. Although I was disqualified for breaking the lane in the 800 meters race, the overall cultural experience of Cuba was indeed enriching.

My family was my main source of support and this was the key of my achievements in sports and in my academic pursuits. I finished high school with seven "GCE, O'Levels," also known as the Cambridge Examination, an English- based examination headquartered in London, England. Grenadian high school students were required to take this examination because our country had been governed by the British prior to our national independence. This was the main exit examination from high school.

After high school, I was employed by the Grenada Board of Education as a Literature and Physical Education Teacher in the St Rose Modern Secondary School. During this time I began contemplating leaving Grenada, to forge the way for a bettter life for my baby and her father in America.   Based on the information I gathered from my half-sisters living in the United States, I made a determination to attend college in Brooklyn, New York. Armed with only a visitor's visa, I was ignorant of the difficult road that lay ahead, and especially of the challenges that would emerge within the family which would welcome me to the United Sates. Not knowing the truth behind the false pretense would eventually lead to wasted years and set backs in my life.

Leaving my daughter Jamillia behind, in the care of my mother and my sister Joycelyn, who was the backbone in raising my child. It was a difficult decision, although Jamillia's dad was present, nevertheless making such a decision was very hard for me because a baby needs his or her mother regardless. Nevertheless, I had the blessings of my mother and my grandmother to take advantage of this chance of a life-time. Sometimes second chances never resurfaced again. However, it would soon become apparent that my great ambitions, hopes and aspiration to reach for the stars, beginning with college attendance, my well-being and sibling relationship would be severely tested.

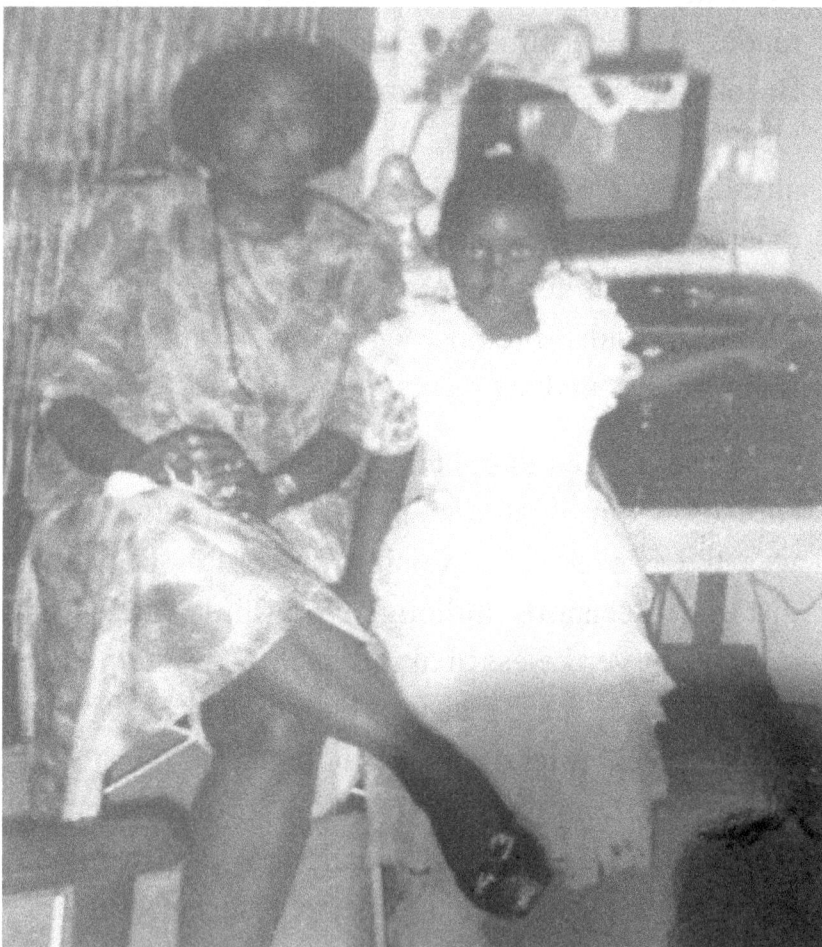

Mom Mavis & Daughter Jamillia

Chapter Two

Goodbyes

It was a hot and humid summer morning, when mommy hugged me with tears streaming down her face, as she said goodbye. It was one of the most painful moments I endured in my life. Leaving my loved-ones behind, especially my thirteen months old baby for the unknown was the hardest thing I ever did. My infant had no idea what was happening, although she was watching and looking sad. I picked her up and squeezed her real tight, kissed her and said goodbye, not knowing that it would take me nine long painful years to lay eyes on her again.

In July of 1988, I departed from the beautiful island of Grenada, which I still call home; I was only 23 years old, as I boarded an American Airlines Jet from Point- a-Saline International Airport bound for Brooklyn, New York. I knew that I was going into the unknown with high expectations, but I was unprepared for challenges and hardship I would encounter in the United States. Most of all, I was unaware how long it would take me to see my mother, baby and my baby's father again. As a matter of fact I never saw my mother   alive again, from that morning when I walked away from her with tears rolling down my face.   Up to this day, this is the last memory I had of my mom.   Losing my mother and not seeing her ever again left an emptiness in my heart.   A hole that cannot be filled but that's part of the cost for migrating to America.

The decision to relinquish my teaching job in Greanada, on July 26th 1988 and head for America in hope of a brighter future for my mother , Mavis, my daughter, Jamillia and her father, Alston, changed my life forever. I heard things were better in America so I decided to take my chances with the encouragement from my family. With a great deal of sadness I left behind my thirteen-month old daughter Jamillia in the care of my mother, grand mother, sister and her father in search of a better future. In the back of my mind I knew someday I will go back to get my baby, so she will have a better life ahead of her. I departed from the beautiful island with white sandy beaches and beautiful blue sea water for a life, that woud eventually prove to be full of peril and disappointments. The belief of securing a future in the American dream, which would eventually trickle down to my baby and her daddy was farfeteched. From the moment the doors of the airline closed, I was unaware that, unknowingly, I was making the most regrettable decision of my life. Naively I lost my mom and my relationship that very said day. Anyway, since I received the blessings from my mother and grandmother when I was departing the land of spice, sunshine and warmth to embark on my journey to the United States of America, I felt at peace within me. I cherished their words of wisdom everyday. Although it was a bitter-sad moment saying goodbyes, when I finally landed in JFK International Airport, I was excited and happy. That excitement, however, was short-lived. The hype ended sharply and bitterly.

The first couple of months were enjoyable and invigorating. I tried to familiarize myself with the city and secure a job, but disillusionment stepped in as soon as I landed a job, and became an ongoing aspect of the life as an immigrant in the United states of America. Life was difficult and at times,unbearable.It was physically and emotionally demanding, but I kept my faith in God and my mother's words of wisdom to hold on and fight. I was determine to reach my goal despite the challenges and disappointments of the journey. At times I reached the point of giving up but I kept hearing my mother's voice saying, "Sharon don't give up; stay focused and be determined, you need to have faith as a grain of mustard seed." I often think that better was ahead, nothing good came without a price. Mom also said, " Sharon, try to remember your purpose for migrating to America. When times get too difficult, think of your baby and me. I also remember my granny saying, "The moment you think of giving up, could be the end of the trials and tribulations." I kept these words in my mind day in and day out until I finally got where I wanted to be. However, before I got there, I went throught the trials of my life. The difficulties I endured as an immigrant in America were unimaginable and heartbreaking but I never gave up hope. I remained determined to reach my goal. I never allowed myself to get sided-tracked and caught up with the wrong company because I kept God and my mom's memories close to my heart. Making the decision to leave Grenada in search of a better future stayed in my mind regardless how hard it became. Although no one told me the truth, I always felt life in America was easy due to my lack of knowledge but as I lived I learned the hard truth on my own.

Chapter Three

Sibling Terror

When I arrived in Brooklyn, New York I was mesmerized by the beauty, the large crowded streets, and the large number of automobiles that flooded the streets; it was love at first sight. The first three months were great; I had fun, sightseeing, partying, eating out and also, gaining weight. Although it seemed endless at the time, it was really short-lived. I was living with my three half-siblings, with whom I share the same father. My experience wth them, caused me to see them as my greatest adversaries, as they were unbelievably evil but within my heart I still had love for them.

We went to church every Sunday, which I looked forward too. However, I also enjoyed going dancing because it was good for my mental health, but my eldest sister was very disapproving of this activity and would call my mom in Grenada to express her concerns about my safety. (Indeed there were known incidents of violence and murder at parties in Brooklyn.) This caused my mother to become agitated and worried about my safety as well but worrying her unecessarily was silly. What happens in Brooklyn should stay there.

Another source of contention was having my mail opened and read by my sibling. The moment I voiced my objections to her reading my mail and making reports to my mother, I was asked to vacate the apartment.   I believe, however, the underlying motive was jealousy. I had obtained a job, with a very nice Jewish family, with whom I had great favor and was blooming ..... The young couple, Dr Hillel and Tammar Bryk, were really good persons—and they were like the family I never had in New York City. They offered and undertook to sponsor me to obtain a green card, so that I could become a legal resident in the United States. (The process took eight years to complete.) They were the kindest and most loving couple I ever met, and   I loved them with every fiber of my being.   I will never forget them.   I loved working with them, and through all my hard times they never gave up on me.

I think God placed me with the Bryks for a reason. Yes, God knows and sees all things. Dr. Hillel and Tammy Bryk   have the biggest hearts ever; they are the most loving parents I ever met besides my mother.   I love them for always and forever.   They are my family and I felt blessed getting to know them.   They had the cutest baby

17

boy I had ever seen; his name was Darren. After two and a half years, they had three other beautiful children, Samantha, Andrew and Bradley whom I partly raised. I love them all, even to point of considering them my children. The good treatment I received fom my employers could have also created a jealous feelings among my step family.

Not only was I asked to leave my siblings' apartment, but the relationship between us deteriorated. There was a cruel attempt, perpetrated by my elder sister January to cause me to lose my job. She concocted a story, which she relayed to my employer, of me being arrested for drug possession after a police raid of the apartment and discovery of drugs in my possession. My employers, out of their concern for me, tried to get someone to handle the processing of the bail-release petition. Their observance of the sabbath prevented them from personally taking actions on my behalf. There was absolutely no basis for this report and at the time this false allegation was being made I was sitting in the livingroom of my step-sisters' apartment watching television, oblvious to the fact they they were plotting my demise. The extent of their relentless and cruel plotting was unfathomable; I am confident that I did nothing to harm or wrong them. Certainly, I did nothing to anyone to deserve this treatment. The only "offensive action" on my part was requesting that my oldest sister respect my privacy with respect to my personal mail. I was asked to leave the apartment on a cold winter's night and with no place to go. They conceeded to my spending the night, a Friday night, before leaving.

On Saturday morning, I left my siblings' apartment, and went to my aunt's house. It was during a call to my employers to inform them of my misfortune and provide a new telephone contact, that I learned about my step-sister's attempt to discredit me so I would be fired. My employer was genuinely concerned; he knew based on his professional expertise as a medical doctor that I was not a drug-user. He had correctly concluded that a false claim was being made against me, but they followed through to get me released from jail. The entire situation was a total fabrication: I was never arrested, nor have I ever smoked, yet because of pure hatred, my step-sister intended to hurt me. I chose to forgive in view of the fact that my step-sister had shown kindness to me in the beginning. Out of respect for the father whom we share and because of my faith in God, I purposed not to hold her actions against her. She and the other two allowed hate to blind them to the fact that their actions against me, would also affect my child and other family members who were depenent upon my financial support.

This episode caused me to be even more grateful to Almighty God for the wonderful employers He had given to me. They were able to make a correct evaluation of my character because of my conduct during the period of service to their child (at that time for six months); they trusted me. It was hard for me to reconcile the evil acts of my step-sisters with their regular church attendance in practice of their Christian faith. I never smoked a cigarette in my life, much less to try drugs. Their actions portrayed them as very mean-spirited and vicious. Their actions sharpened my resolve to always deal with others with love and compassion. America is a place that makes or breaks an individual. One has to have strength and faith in Amighty God in order to persevere to the end because friends and family change and become evil in America. This is truly a really sad indictment. Individuals who allow themselves to be influenced by jealousy are under the control of the devil, who uses this as an avenue to take possession of their minds, bodies and souls thus engaging them in wicked acts against others. The goodness of God stands as a counterforce against such evil, as he surrounds you with those with whom you have favor and who can vouch for your integrity. God works wonders and never allows someone to bear more than his or her fair share. That is why God brings wonderful people into our lives.

Celebrating Jamillia's 9th Birthday in a New Home

Chapter Four

More Family Woes

After my relatives forced me to leave their apartment, I went to live with my aunt Bessie, which turned out to be another big mistake. She had a small studio apartment, which she subdivided to separate the bedroom from the living room. I hated living with her because I had no privacy--I slept on her couch in the open hall with her pet cat, named Ginger, whose hair was all over the place. Beyond that, there was something frightening about Ginger. The moment I stepped into the apartment on weekends (I remained at my place of employment during the week) Ginger would stand at the bedroom door, intimidating me with his intense stare and making me feel extremely uncomfortable. He behaved like the watchman for the apartment. I wanted to chase him away but I was so intimidated by his penetrating stare that I believed he would pounce on me in retaliation.

Whenever my aunt was preparing to cut Ginger's toe nails, she tried to enlist me to assist her by holding Ginger's paws, but I was so scared I could neither watch him nor touch his paws. She would then be forced to take   him to the pet groomers. I realized I was being resentful of that cat, because of its bold, intimidating stare which was particularly frightening at nights. My aunt, on the other hand, was totally enamored with Ginger, to the point of considering him her baby. She was constantly referring to him as Ginger this and Ginger that.   I do not consider myself a cat-friendly person, so this was a very challenging situation, but I refrained from telling my mom what I was going through. On a more positive side, I enjoyed a few months of quietude while staying at aunt's. Then, suddenly the relationship between my aunt and myself started turning sour.

It began when I requested that Aunt Bessie open a joint savings account with both our names. This evidently was displeasing to Auntie Bessie, who had been keeping my finances in her checking acccount. Soon, Aunt Bessie started mistreating me. She and her husband had meals without offering any portion to me, in spite of my weekly contribution of fifty dollars to cover my living expenses. At that time, I was earning one hundred and fifty dollars per week; had a child and other family members to take care of in Grenada. She informed me that meals were not covered by my weekly contributions. I purposed that neither her attitude nor that of my step-sisters would deter me from pursuing my goals.

Then she launched into complaints about the difficulties she experienced in America, which included, sleeping on the floor. Whilst I could sympathize with her feelings, I was also mindful that times had changed and that her experience need not be replicated in my life. However, I held my peace, listened and forced my mind to remain correctly focused.

These painful experiences in New York City caused me to regret leaving my good teaching job, my mom, my daughter Jamillia and my boyfriend to pursue a better life in America. Night after night I would cry, but I prayed for strength, courage and faith to go on. With Gods's grace I held on.

While living with my aunt I made friends with the neighbors, the Rodrick, who were really nice people; they were also from Grenada. I started going to church with them on Sundays. They would also invite me to join them for the Sunday meal; then I would return to my job in Queens on Sunday night. At this point in my life, I was very sad and depressed but continued to hold on for the future of my daugter Jamillia because at this point I have lost my baby's daddy and my mom and Grand mother. I stayed with my aunt for almost six months, but my trials continued. In the end, she abandon the apartment with my belongings still inside.

In November of 1990, my aunt called me at work to inform me that she had obtained a one-bedroom apartment and that I was responsible for paying half the rent. This seemed unfair to me, since with 3 persons living in the apartment; and additionally, I would be there only on week-ends. She made it clear that if I didn't agree to her terms, I would have to make my own arrangements. That same Wednesday, before Thanksgiving, I returned to Brooklyn with the hopes of spending Thanksgiving with my aunt and her husband. To my complete surprise, upon entering the studio apartment, I discovered it was empty except for my suitcase in one corner of the room My aunt and her husband had moved out without calling to inform me. This was devastating, as I had nowhere to go and it was cold, with a great deal of snow on the ground. I cried. About about half an hour later, I regained my composure, left the empty apartment and went across the street to speak with Mrs Eunice Rodrick and her husband about my predicatment. They suggested that I store my suitcase in their basement and spend the night. I hardly slept that night; it seemed that my life was falling apart, with the exception of my job, for which I was truly grateful to Almighty God.

Then the next day which was Thanksgiving day, I informed my employers about my predicament. My employers, the Bryks, were wonderful during my time of need; as a result my love for them deepened. When I started working with the family, I was very happy, as they were my age group. They had one child; an adorable baby boy. I instantly fell in love with family, and still love them today. They were, and still are, like family to me. I could not expect better from strangers. I worked with them for nine years and when I decided to go back to school, they were very supportive. When my daughter Jamillia came to live in America she also stayed at their home with me. They are the most genuinely sincere people I ever met in New York City. They were honest with me and I thank God for knowing them and getting into their lives. They were very helpful when my aunt turned against me. That Wednesday night I was so depressed and saddened that my own flesh and blood could deal so heartlessly with me. It seemed to me that something about America caused drastic changes in people and relationships. I made a vow then, never to change my kind ways towards my family and friends.

On Thanksgiving day, I also informed my cousin about my changed circumstances: that I had nowhere to stay because my aunt moved out without informing me. My cousin Majorie Chase invited me to come and live with her family, but I agreed only to leave my belongings with them, after which I went back on my job in Queens. I stayed for three months on my job but visited Brooklyn from time to time, until I was able to rent a single room there. I moved into the room because I wanted to give the family I was working with space on the weekend. Although the Bryks were welcoming, I did not want to overstay my welcome. Every Friday evening I left for the weekend to go to my rented room in Brooklyn, still feeling sad and lonely. I stayed in that room for six years before I got an apartment. The memories of unpleasant experiences living with family members caused me to vow, that I would no longer live with any family members until my daughter arrived in America.

Unfortunately, my hardships didn't come to an end. The most deverstating blow during my sojourn in the United States of America was yet to come. It felt like a horror movie without an end.

Sharon and Jamillia Stages of Graduation

Sharon Associate Degree: Jamillia High School

Chapter Five

The Fateful Mother's Day

It was Mothers' day on May 9th 1993, when I spoke to Mommy. She was happy, healthy and joyful celebrating Mothers' day with the rest of the family. I was sad because I wasn't there but she reassured me that it we would soon be together. I dearly missed mommy and the rest of the family, but talking to her on the phone helped me to stay close as possible to them, especially my baby. It was hard for me but I tried to stay brave for my mother. I loved my mother with all my heart and I just could not believe what transpired next.

It was the morning of May 10th 1993 following Mother's day, around nine o'clock, while I was at work, that the devasting phone call came informing me that my mom could not speak. Mrs Bryk answered the phone and her facial expression made me want to speak to my mom immediately. I didn't know that she was already dead. Mrs Bryk told me to use the phone in the bedroom, so I did. When I called Grenada to speak to my mother, it was Ms Jean Duncan who answered the phone; this was puzzling to me: why was she answering the phone?. I asked to speak to mommy and I was told, mommy is unable to speak. At first I thought it was a prank. Then I said "put the phone by her ear so I can speak to her." Then, the neighbor said she can not speak because she died. At the sound of these words I ran out of the house and I fell on the grass. When I recovered it was almost mid-day. I was given some medication to help me keep calm, as this was a terrible situation for me. My green card had not yet been issued as the immigration application was still being processed. I did not realize that I could have obtained emergency travel documents, and my attorney made no attempts to help me.

I screamed and kept screaming; I felt I was going crazy. My employers didn't know who to call at the moment because I had no one except my cousin. I told them I wanted to go to my room in Brooklyn. They put me in a cab and saw me off. I remained there for a week until the burial of my mother was completed. It was really hard but I was praying that I would not get a nervous break down. My daughter was all I could think of because my mother was her mommy—that's how she related to her. Mommy would not be there any more therefore, she will be losing another mother. It was a really difficult time, but a couple of friends I made came to visit me and one of them, Judy, in an act of generosity, paid my rent for that week. At that moment it had been 5 years since I had seen my mother, my baby and my baby's father. I felt like a wreak, but I kept praying to God for strength so I would not go crazy. I placed the entire situation in the hands of God. It was the most horrible feelings to have. Losing my mother whom I hadn't seen for five years and would not be able to see for the rest of my life was the worst experience ever. A deep void remains with me even today.

It took me months to realize that she was really gone. It took me a couple of years to acceept the fact that Mommy is really dead. I had the funeral service video-taped so I could watch with the hope of getting closure. Closure took years because every time I started watching the video, I would cry. After four or five years, I stopped watching the video in order to heal. Making the decision to come to America in search of a better future really came with a great cost, but I was determined to continue to work towards my goals, which included getting my Green card, having my daughter Jamillia residing with me, going back to school and, getting married.

Losing my mom was the most devastating blow I experienced while living in the United States. I became withdrawn. I lost my appetite and started losing weight. In a matter of one month I went from a size sixteen to a size ten. I could not socialize. I felt like my world was falling apart. I had a few friends who tried to help me. I had no close family at this time, so I was basically alone.

The greatest loss for me in my life was losing my mother. I came to the USA to make a life for my baby and my mother. I really wanted her to come to America but God had other plans in store for her. I tried not to question it but for years I just could not get over it. I kept hearing her last words to me, "Wait until you get your papers, then you can come and see me." That day never came for us to meet or see each other.   I wanted my mom to see America. She had never been to the USA, so I wanted to give her that opportunity but God said "No" and took her away, leaving me empty, without closure. Mommy was my best friend and a good mother. I loved her and I missed her dearly. I could talk to mommy about anything. Even now, today, I still find it hard to believe she left us. My mom was 58 years old when God took her from us, but still I do not have closure because I was unable to attend her furneal. Being close to my mom made it very difficult for me to accept that she died. For years I believed she hadn't died,

Two years before I lost my mother, I lost my grand mother. My Grandmother died of a heart attack, just like my mom. My granny died in her sleep. She went to bed and she never woke up. My mom was going down the street and she collasped and died. My world came apart because I was very close with my mother and she and my younger sister was raising my baby. I was the only one that had some money to pay for the burial expenses; no one else in the family had any money to bury her. I had been taking care of her and the rest of the family financially. I sent the money to take care of the burial, but I could not attend. I bought the dress for her to be buried in. It was very difficult to deal with the purchase of the dress and the gloves. I cried in the store and all the way home knowing that I had just bought a dress to bury my mother, who I had not seen for five long years. God knows best, but I just could not understand why he took her from us at the age of 58. This experience I will never wish it on my worst enemy. Losing a mother is the hardest loss to endure; it is not an easy thing.

After losing my mother I had to redirect my attention to my baby because, although I had my brothers and sisters, she was all I really had. I tried to focus on my baby who was now six years old and doing well with the help of my sister Joycelyn her third mother. I thank God Joycelyn was there to take over after mom passed. However, Her dad was there in her life, so she was alright because at least one of her parents was always with her. I spoke to her on the phone weekly, and sometimes daily. I started praying and asking God to give me strength, courage, and faith to hang on. Trusting in God gave me strength to hold on and keep fighting to get my immigration papers so I would be able to see my baby and have her join me in the United States of America.

I started serving God and praying harder, with the hope that nothing else would happen, as I could not handle any more disappointments. I felt my life in the USA was not going anywhere, that bad things were happening too frequently. I asked God through my prayers to give me a chance to see my baby before she celebrated her tenth birthday. Yes, God answered my prayers. It was a blessing to finally see my baby girl three years after my mom died.

It was in June of 1995 that I received a call from my attorney, informing me that my immigration papers had come through and I needed to sign the final papers. I started screaming with joy and sorrow. I was going to see my baby but, I would also be visiting the grave of my mother. It was a heartbreaking and joyful moment at the same time. I fell to my knees and expressed my deep apppreciation for the work of GOD in my life. These bitter-sweet moments seemed to be always present in my life but, God knows best. He gives and He takes away. I praised and thanked Him, as He is deserving. He was there with me through all the challenges I had encountered during my time in the United States.

In June 1995 I was given my work permit and social security card. I completed all the paper work and returned them to my attorney. In

September 1995, after eight long years in Amereica, I visited Grenada. (Yes it took me eight years to become a legal resident). I went to see my baby who was now eight years old. It was a joy to see her. I knew I lost many years in her life, but I was determined to make up for that. I took her back to America in March 1996, a dream come through, amidst the ongoing trials and tribulations. I wept with joy.

At this point in time I was renting a one bedroom apartment in a private building in the Flatbush section of Brooklyn. It was a decent apartment but, the management services were sub-standard, failing to follow through with routine repairs, concerned only with collecting rent promptly on the due date. At one point I was forced to take my landlord to court to get my apartment painted. I had lived there for eight years, kept my apartment clean, but there was a clear need to have it painted. The judge for the housing court ordered the landlord to paint the apartment and do other repairs. Today, after living there for 15 years, I still experience the same challenges, but now I enlist the authority of the court to work on my behalf.

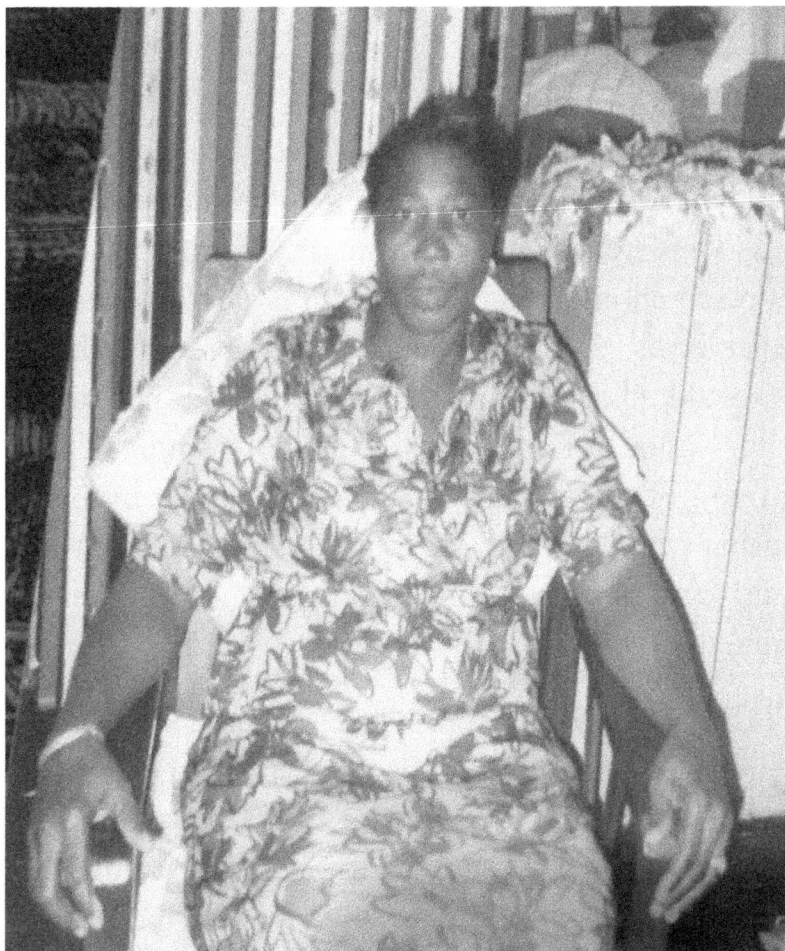

Mavis Frederick née Charles

Chapter Six

Medical Nightmares

On October 3rd 2002, I faced a medical challenge-fibroids, a huge tumor plus many small ones, were revealed during medical exam. I did my research and found an OBGYN doctor, who I will refer as "Dr. Stonesoup." He assured me that he would take care of the fibroids. I had the surgery done at Long Island College Hospital. The morning of the surgery I was accompanied by my cousin, who was the only family member that I could call upon, as the other relationships were strained.

All I remembered was lying on a cold steel bed in the operating room and a nurse wearing a mask instructing me to take a deep breath. Sometime later, I woke up to see another nurse standing at my bedside, who instructed me to press the "call button" if I experienced pain. I was amazed that everything happened so fast, and that I was alive. This was my first surgical procedure; and it seemed to me that everything went well. I was assigned to a semi-private room, with one other patient. I spent a couple of days in the hospital while my daughter stayed with Joycelyn.

After completing my first follow-up visit with "Dr. Stonesoup", I tried to schedule a second follow-up appointment. I was told that, the doctor was no longer accepting my insurance. (I had HIP Insurance at the time). Devastated and frustrated, I searched for an answer, but decided not to pursue the matter. At that point I didn't understand the underlying cause of his refusal to continue accepting me as a patient. I was feeling fine and therefore, saw no reason to pursue the matter.

After seven years I came to the realization that the doctor had been covering up his mistakes. He had used the wrong sutures during the surgery, which caused the stitches to remain in my abdomen, instead of melting away. Perhaps he was scared that I would discover his blunder and take actions against him. One evening after taking a shower and while drying my skin, I noticed a blue piece of string hanging out of my belly. I started screaming and yelling. The next morning I went to the emergency room at Methodist Hospital in Brooklyn and I was told, there were sutures in my abdomen. I was freaking out; this was disastrous. I was told, I had to make another appointment to have the sutures removed or that I should go back to the doctor who performed the sugery.

Being naïve I went back to "Dr. Stonesoup." He tried cutting off the piece of stitches that was protruding from my abdomen, but I realizing he was trying to cover up his mistake and not do the right thing, I refused to have this done. That same night he called me and told me he was willing to help me. Inexplicably, I believed him because I still trusted and liked him because I believed him to be a very good OBGYN doctor. I did not, nor could not believe, that this was a set-up. I had no-one to turn to for advice and I trusted "Dr. Stonesoup". I was grateful that he helped me by removing the fibroids, one which I was told, was as big as a grapefruit. I understand that mistakes do happen but, this doctor went beyond that—he betrayed my trust.

So when "Dr. Stonesoup" called to inform me that he wanted me to meet a surgeon, who would examine the stitches to determine what method should be used to remove them, I agreed to the meeting. However, this was soon revealed to be an attempt to camouflage his error.

It is evident to me that the doctors took advantage of me because of my naïvety, ignorance and lack of experience in America.   "Dr.

Stonesoup" arranged for me to consult with "Dr. Riversnake." At this meeting, Dr. Riversnake asked me to lay on the examination bed so he could have a look. Then, suddenly and without warning, this wicked "Dr. Riversnake" started pulling the stitches out of my belly. This was very painful, as the stitches were embedded within my flesh. I screamed in pain, then I asked him what he was doing. He laughed in my face and informed me that he had just cut off the stitches. I was petrified. I could not believe what Dr. Riversnake did. He simply wanted to cover up the evidence to help his friend not me. He didn't conduct a consultation. I wanted all the stiches to be removed from my body; they could have done it the right way, not simply cutting off the protruding ends that were visible.

I had no one to help me, so again I turned to the courts for help. As I was unable to retain the services of an attorney, I went to the civil court on Livingston Street and filed a petition against both doctors for betraying my trust. The lawyers whom they hired to represent them tried to get the case dismissed. "Dr. Stonesoup's" defense lawyer got the case dismissed based on the statute of limitation, as three years had already passed. However, there is a clause that allows the plaintiff to file a suit when a problem is discovered. The case was nonetheless dismissed, I believe because the defense bribed the court attorney, who was representing me.

The case against "Dr. Riversnake" was going well, but my case was dismissed, again, I believe, because the defense paid the Judge and the Court attorney to dismiss my case. On appeal I won the case, because, although they filed a counter-motion, they failed to respond. The judge in the inquest, I believe was also bribed to interfere with the outcome of the case. I had filed for thirty thousand ($30,000) but the judge added twenty thousand dollars ($20,000), making a total of fifty thousand dollars ($50,000), which is beyond the financial limit of this court's jurisdiction in civil court. Hence, my case was dismissed.

It is evident to me that the court sytem took advantage of me, because I could not afford an attorney. Since the statute of limitation had expired no attorney wanted the case because they could not get a lump sum of money for themselves.

For me, the issue was more that of betrayal of trust, than monetary compensation. I believe the court system is corrupted: it is all about greed, not helping people in the pursuit of justice, it is not about doing the right thing. I took the doctors to court for the wrong they had done to me, but the court allowed them to get away with it because of the voice of money. I believe that the judge is morally corrupt, and will answer to the Higher Authority of Almighty GOD, for all the wrongs done to innocent honest immigrants like myself.

The defense attorney offered to pay me three hundred dollars in front of the court attorney; they wanted me to accept three hundred dollars in exchange for dropping all charges against the doctor. Why would the defense attorney try to bribe me with three hundred dollars? I refused. The court attorney was very corrupt; he and the Judge will receive their own retribution judgement from Almighty God. They will suffer the consequences of their actions before they leave this world. Nothing goes unpaid. God is merciful.

The series of court designated hearings between December 15, 2010 at 141 Livingston Street, Brooklyn, dismissal of individuals assisting me etc. have led me to conclude that the Brooklyn court sytem is corrupt. Persons like myself, who are immigrants with little financial resources to retain the services of an attorney, are unlikely to see a just resolution of their cases. However, as no man is a pillar, these corrupt officials will experience the retribution of GOD, unless they make amends. Judgement day is ahead and they must give account to God for what they did to me.

As March 2011 I still have stitches in my belly and the protruding portion is not visible. It seems my body was rejecting the stitches. They used the wrong type of stitches, they had to use suture that dissolve but instead they used the blue plastic ones.   I do not believe their medical practices will last forever. They will reap what they have sown. After this ordeal had passed, I tried to put it behind me and continue to focus on completing my degree, but there was yet another challenging situation to be dealt with.

Chapter Seven

Insurance Horrors

On August 7th 2010, I was in a minor car accident. The driver of the car didn't include my name in the police report. Before the police arrived on the scene of the accident, I was taken by the ambulance to the hospital, so I could be attended to immediately as my shoulder was hurting and feeling numb. Since I had an underlying condition, "High Blood Pressure", the ambulance personnel didn't want to wait until the police arrived. After the accident, I was home for one week. The driver didn't come to the hospital, nor did he call to see how I was feeling.

kAfter three weeks of pain and finally getting the police report, I realized that the driver had omitted my name. I tried to get the officer that did the report to amend it but was unable to locate him. I had to use insurance provided by my job to go to my doctor for follow-ups. However, Blue Cross and Blue Sheild refused to pay the hospital bill, placing the responsibility on the driver's insurance. Since the driver refused to put my name on the report, the insurance did not pay the bill. I had to work something out with the hospital to take care of the bill. Medicaid was not going to pay because I had Blue Cross and Blue Sheild. I was left in the rain.

I had not filed any insurance claims, however, upon the driver's report of my injuries to his insurance company, a no-fault claim was filed in my name—but without informing me. Yet, the driver still refused to include my name in the police report. About this time, I realized that I was being kept under surveillance. There was someone following me every day. They followed me to church, the store, the laundromat, school, work , shopping, everywhere. They looked at me, but said nothing. I had no idea what was behind their actions. I tried confronting them, but they continued to follow me without saying a word. In the beginning, I was scared, I wasn't able to eat, drink, study or sleep.

I was working on my Bachelor's degree in Education at Medgar Evers College therefore, I had to drop out that semester. I was terrified when I first noticed these people were following me. It seems to be an attempt to intimidate me, which was inexplicable, as I had not filed any injury claims. The surveillance continued, even during the cold winter months; persons would sit in their cars and watch me. When I pretended not to see them, they would take some action to get my attention, such as revving up their engine, or blowing the horn of their vehicles. I did my best to ignore them. Three years later, they still have me under surveillance.

I contacted the police many times, but was informed that there were no grounds for an arrest; I did not have a face nor a name to file a report. I found the situation tireseome and annoying, but decided to trust God all through this ordeal. I prayed constantly and trusted God. I wrote the district councilman, who contacted the police department,who in turn contacted me. Now I hope they will help to get to the bottom of this situation. Being kept under constant observation, being followed everywhere on a 24 hour basis, every day, has been very disturbing and unnerving. At times, I would ask God why He had brought me to this country to endure so many trials and tibulations, while hoping the outcome would be alright.

Certainly, the individual or individuals behind this surveillance had a motive, which was hidden from me. The positive aspect of this is that I prayed constantly and never leave the house without asking for the help of Almighty God. I had worked so hard to get to this level of achievement, and although I desire to own a home, I am satisfied with my accomplishments thus far. It seems that there was someone lurking in the shadows that was determined to destroy my happiness and my life. Nonetheless I remained strong in The Lord. I felt at one point I was getting a nervous breakdown from this ordeal. During that point in time, I began to sense an unusual odor from my hair or breath. Despite visiting different doctors for a solution, none was found. I was told it was my mind and that I needed to sleep. I rejected these explanations but no medical doctors had a definite answer.

In August of 2010, I was feeling depressed and ashamed by the hateful comments people made every time I left home to go to work, church or the store. For instance, on the bus people would sniff or move away from me. No one would sit near to me. It seems to me that people were smelling something in my hair or on my breath, even though I was not speaking. At one point, I felt like quitting my job and staying home, where no one would see me; that is how bad it was, but I prayed and continued to fast. With God on my side I didn't quit my job. I continued going to different doctors and dentists but their reassurances were not helping me. At one point a doctor gave me a precription for medication to help me sleep, which I refused to take. I also saw a psychiatrist, who attempted to load me up with medication. I refused to take any of these psychiatric medication because I know the outcome of these medications. I decided to take things in strides, living one day at a time.

The greatest support for me in the USA came from Michael Samuel, the Bryk family—Tammy and Hillel, their children Darren, Bradley Andrew and my "pussycat" Sammy D. I love them dearly. God chose them for me; our paths were destined to cross. Their support was especially powerful during this disturbing situation as I tried to remain focused on completing my Bachelor's degree in Education. I also continued to pray and fast. I needed to be there for my daughter also because she too was in college. Having decided that no one would stop me from achieving my desired goal or destroy my life, it was especially heartening to read Andrew Bryk's letter. Andrew was one of my babies; I nicknamed him "Pepperseed". He was one of the four children I baby-sat in my first job. "Pepperseed" wrote a letter for me on his birthday because he was concerned about me and my situation concerning the smell. He wanted to reassure me that there was nothing wrong with me. He wrote:

"Sharon Charles - Our Hero

As you have closed in on 50 and yet still look 25, all I can say to you Sharon is how amazing you have been for our family. Ever since you left Grenada at a young age to pursue the American dream, you met little Darren and my parents, and laid down the famous ground rules; The location of Timeout", the speed at which you counted 1...2...3, and the amount of food you needed to shove down our throats because apparently my parents had trouble feeding us. I don't know what my childhood would have been like without you.

I cannot imagine what it would be like to leave my family's home to move to another country to gain a better life. There is so much that you have taught me. You were a world class runner at the Central American & Caribbean Games, something I wish I could have seen you participate in. But I must say, you were also a world class babysitter and friend in the Bryk household, and this I was lucky to see. You have been a part of so many key moments in my life. Some of my most amazing memories include you. An example of the love you displayed all the times you loved taking me to the park to play and get ice cream.

Sharon, you were somehow able to keep 3 crazy boys from killing each other, while also trying to take care of and look after the cutest little girl. I do not know how you did it but all I can say is that it was incredible.

After you moved on from staying with us, you have only become more of a hero to me. You continued to take classes and learn to move up your profession. You are always working your hardest and even though you may want to give up at times, you never do. You will pass your tests next year and don't let anyone tell you otherwise. You do not smell, and you do not have bad breath, and it is normal to get nervous and anxious. We all do!! You have done all of this while raising Jamilia, who has gone on to have great success. Sharon, you may be 50 but I write this to you to tell you that you have accomplished so much and will continue to grow even more. I cannot be more appreciative for what you have given me and my family. You are truly a part of the Bryk family.

We will always be there for you at all times and all you need to know is that you can do it, because you are our hero."

Love you,
Andrew (peppaseeda)

At Church in Brooklyn

Chapter Eight

My University Education

It is January 2013. I am still being followed by the unknown observer; it seems this will continue indefinitely. I continued to ignore it, confident that someday this would come to an end, even after four years of observing my every move. I thought of hiring a private investigator to help but, decided it was not worth the expenditure of valuable resources, which I needed to complete my degree program and pay my bills. Most importantly, I am nearing the completion of my goal and I hope with health and strength I will cross the finish line despite the hardships, headaches and set-backs I had experienced along the way. I stayed positive, stayed away from bad influences and stayed true to myself.

It is currently 2014 and I have completed one semester of my teaching practice. On January 27th 2014, I will begin the spring semester focusing on "student teaching practice," with the expectation of graduating in June 2014 with my Bachelor's degree. From my humble beginnings as a baby sitter in New York City, and with perserverance, courage and the help of God, together with the words of my mom, the help from Mr Michael Samuel, I will obtain a Bachelor 's degree—one of my main reason for coming to America. I am excited, but sad because neither my mom nor my older brother Oswald or sister Cecelyn will be here to share the moment with me. I would love for them to be here, but unfortunately, they had not been called by the immigration office for their visa interviews as yet.

I filed for them to become permenant residents, but after ten years they have yet to be called. In any case, my daughter Jamillia, my sister Joycelyn marlene Ledford and my best friend Michael Samuel will share the moment with me. Unfortunately the Bryk family won't be able to attend due to the observance of their sabbath but I know they all will be there in spirit along with my dear mother Mavis Charles nee Frederick. The day I hoped for from the moment I set foot in the United States of America. The dream of a life time. The dream I will never forget.

Chapter 9

Optimism Despite All

Most importantly, my outlook on the future had been very optimistic and I worked towards fulfilling my goals despite the hardships, trials and misfortunes. I always wanted to make my family proud especially, my mother and I think I did just that. Although she is not here to share the moment, she will be smiling, wherever she is. I obtained my Green Card and now I am a United States Citizen; my daughter is also a citizen. I graduated with my Associate degree in Childhood Education in 2006, but presently I am a senior in college and will have a Bachelor in Childhood Education and a minor in Social Science. My daughter has completed college and has her Bachelor's degree in allied Health from St John's University. She also completed her Master's Degree in Hospital Management at Long Island University.

Although I had a difficult and challenging experience, with my trust in and the strength from the Almighty Father above, the wonderful professors at Medgar Evers College, supportive friends/employer, I faced the storms and did my best in the United States. I knew for sure my mom is smiling down on us because I stayed determined and accomplished my goals. Although it took a long time, it is "better to be late than never," as the popular saying goes. No matter how the odds were stacked against me, God was there for me. I gather my courage and lifted my spirits through this inspirational quote, which is located near my computer at home and in the work place:

> "God grant me the serenity to accept the things I cannot change: Courage to change the things I can; and the wisdom to know the difference." (By Reinhold Niebuhr)

There are many opportunities in America for all immigrants, and staying true to oneself and trusting Almighty God will get them to their final destinations. No one is a mountain, we all need somebody to help us to get where we want to go. I believed in myself and my dream although it seemed unreachable at times in my heart and soul I felt it was definitely achievable in no other place than United States of America.

Jamillia's Master's Graduation

Chapter 10
Success at Last

Finally, on May 31st 2014, I proudly walked across the platform at the Barcklays Center in Brooklyn on Medgar Evers' Commencement day. That was the proudest day of my life, but it was also bitter-sweet because my mother was not there to share that proud moment with me. Nevertheless, my sister Joycelyn, my daughter Jamillia, my best friend Michael and my former employer Ms. Marlene Ledford were there to celebrate with me. I felt blessed because I longed for that day to arrive and finally my dream came through, albeit taking me a long time. Determination and Hope got me where I am today. Now I am pursuing my state certification to become licensed classroom teacher in childhood education K-6. I would like to specialize in Social Studies, therefore, I foresee a Master's degree in my future.

Significantly, I got to the end of the jouney despite the stress and difficulties I endured in the USA. **Despite all odds**, with strength, health, determination, supportive individuals and the grace of God, anyone can fulfill their dream in the United States of America. This is a beautiful country with lots of opportunities. I encourage those on the journey or those whom you know are on the journey to stay motivated and strong, although it may seem dark, gloomy or unreachable at times. Be assured: you will eventually reap the ultimate benefit. I, Sharon D. Charles, just did. Sweet success at last.

Happy Ending

SPINE

Charles   RISING ABOVE ALL ODDS   CDP

www.ingramcontent.com/pod-product-compliance
Lightning Source LLC
Chambersburg PA
CBHW071430040426
42445CB00012BA/1331